THE JOYS OF ONE POT PASTAS

No pre-boiling or draining *(the pasta cooks in the sauce)* • Fewer dirty dishes *(everything cooks in one pot)* • Perfect anytime *(quick & easy – great for a week night or weekend)* • Versatile *(use virtually any type of pasta)* • Simply delicious *(need we say more?)*

Spaghetti, Linguini, Fettuccini

Ravioli (frozen)

Tortellini (frozen)

Printed in the United States of America
by G&R Publishing Co.

Distributed By:

CQ Products

507 Industrial Street
Waverly, IA 50677

ISBN-13: 978-1-56383-500-1
Item #7120

Campanelle

Pipette

Egg Noodles

Rigatoni

Elbows

Rings

Lasagna

Rotini

Old-Fashioned Egg Noodles

Shells

Penne

Ziti

OH THE PASTA-BILITIES...

One Pot Pastas

4 qt. pot

4

SHRIMP & SPINACH LINGUINI

16 oz. uncooked linguini noodles,
  broken in half if desired

1½ lbs. frozen cooked shrimp

1 (14.5 oz.) can diced tomatoes

4 cloves garlic, chopped

1 T. Italian seasoning

¼ C. chopped fresh basil

Juice of 1 lemon

Salt & pepper to taste

4 C. chicken broth

3 oz. fresh baby spinach

TO BEGIN, combine uncooked noodles, frozen shrimp, tomatoes, garlic, Italian seasoning, basil, lemon juice, salt, and pepper in a pot. Stir in broth; bring to a boil. Cook on medium heat for 6 minutes, stirring occasionally to separate noodles. Add spinach. Cook 4 minutes more or until noodles are tender.

SPRINKLE WITH more Italian seasoning. ▌

5

PASTA PRIMAVERA

2 T. olive oil

½ onion, sliced

1 garlic clove, thinly sliced

2 carrots, cut into matchsticks

½ red bell pepper, cut into matchsticks

1 C. frozen peas

2¼ C. half & half

¾ C. chicken stock

Salt & pepper to taste

8 oz. uncooked penne pasta

Zest & juice of ½ lemon

¼ C. chopped fresh parsley

Grated Parmesan cheese

One Pot Pastas

6

TO BEGIN, heat oil in a pot. Add onion and garlic; cook for 2 minutes, stirring constantly. Add carrots, bell pepper, and frozen peas; cook

DIRECTIONS CONTINUED ··························>

2 minutes more, stirring often. Stir in half & half, chicken stock, salt, and pepper; bring to a simmer. Stir in uncooked pasta. Cook for 15 minutes or until pasta is tender, stirring often. Stir in lemon zest, lemon juice, and parsley.

SPRINKLE WITH
Parmesan cheese. ▮

7

One Pot Pastas

3 qt. pot

8

ALL-AT-ONCE
SPAGHETTI

- 1 lb. lean ground beef
- 1 onion, chopped
- 3 (8 oz.) cans tomato sauce
- 1½ C. water
- 1½ tsp. salt
- ¼ tsp. each pepper & garlic powder
- 1¼ tsp. dried oregano
- 8 oz. uncooked spaghetti noodles
- 1¼ C. shredded Cheddar or mozzarella cheese, divided

TO BEGIN, cook ground beef and onion in a pot until done, breaking up meat as it cooks. Stir in tomato sauce, water, salt, pepper, garlic powder, and oregano. Bring to a boil. Add uncooked noodles; reduce heat to a simmer, stirring to separate noodles. Cover tightly and cook for 25 to 30 minutes. Uncover and stir in 1 cup cheese.

SPRINKLE WITH remaining cheese. ∎

9

CRUSTLESS
CHICKEN POT PIE

- 2 T. butter
- 1 onion, chopped
- 1 celery rib, chopped
- 1 tsp. minced garlic
- 8 oz. fresh mushrooms, sliced
- 1 T. flour
- 2 C. water
- 2 tsp. instant chicken bouillon granules
- 1 C. heavy cream
- 2 C. uncooked rigatoni pasta
- 2 C. shredded cooked chicken
- 1 C. frozen veggies of your choice
- 1 T. lemon juice
- 1 tsp. each finely chopped fresh thyme & rosemary
- ¼ tsp. dried sage
- 1½ tsp. salt
- ½ tsp. pepper

TO BEGIN, melt butter in a pot. Add onion, celery, garlic, and mushrooms; cook until golden

DIRECTIONS CONTINUED ·····················>

brown. Sprinkle flour over veggies; cook and stir about 1 minute. Add water, bouillon granules, and cream. Bring to a simmer and slowly dump in uncooked pasta. Simmer for 10 minutes or until liquid has thickened slightly and pasta is al dente, stirring occasionally. Stir in chicken, frozen veggies, lemon juice, thyme, rosemary, sage, salt, and pepper. Cook until heated through.

GARNISH WITH more thyme and rosemary. ∎

11

One Pot Pastas

3 qt. pot

12

SIMPLE GOULASH

2 lbs. lean ground beef

2 tsp. salt

1 tsp. garlic salt

1 tsp. dried oregano

2 T. Italian seasoning

4 (15 oz.) cans tomato sauce

1 (8 oz.) can tomato sauce

3 C. water

1 T. dried minced onion

16 oz. uncooked elbow macaroni

TO BEGIN, brown ground beef in a pot until done, breaking up meat as it cooks. Stir in salt, garlic salt, oregano, Italian seasoning, all the tomato sauce, water, dried onion, and uncooked macaroni. Bring to a boil. Reduce heat and simmer for 20 minutes or until macaroni is tender, stirring occasionally.

GARNISH WITH fresh cilantro and peppers. ∎

13

PASTA WITH
LEEKS &
HAM

2 T. butter

1 T. olive oil

1 C. cubed cooked ham

3 medium leeks,
   sliced & rinsed

2 cloves garlic, finely
   chopped

½ tsp. ground sage

12 oz. uncooked ziti pasta

4 to 5 C. vegetable stock

1½ tsp. lemon pepper

¼ C. chopped fresh parsley

Grated Parmesan cheese

14

PSST, DIRECTIONS HERE···········

makes 6 servings

TO BEGIN, heat together butter and oil in a skillet. Add ham and leeks. Cook for 2 minutes, stirring occasionally. Stir in garlic, sage, and uncooked pasta; cook 2 minutes more, stirring constantly. Pour in enough vegetable stock to just cover pasta. Cover skillet and simmer for 6 minutes. Uncover and cook 3 to 4 minutes more or until pasta is just tender, stirring occasionally. Stir in lemon pepper and parsley.

SPRINKLE WITH cheese and more parsley. ▌

15

16

MEATLESS
SKILLET LASAGNA

1 (12 oz.) pkg. frozen veggie crumbles (such as Morning Star Farms Meal Starters), partially thawed

1 tsp. minced garlic

1 (14.5 oz.) can diced Italian style tomatoes

1 (25 oz.) jar spaghetti sauce

⅔ C. cream of onion soup

½ C. egg substitute

12 oz. cottage cheese

¾ tsp. Italian seasoning

9 uncooked oven-ready lasagna noodles

1 C. each shredded Colby-Jack & mozzarella cheese

TO BEGIN, mix crumbles, garlic, tomatoes, and spaghetti sauce in a bowl. In a separate bowl, mix soup, egg substitute, cottage cheese, and Italian seasoning. Spread 1½ cups spaghetti sauce mixture in a skillet and cover with half the cottage cheese mixture. Add half the noodles (breaking to fit), the remaining cottage cheese, 1½ cups sauce, and remaining noodles. Cover with remaining sauce. Bring to a boil. Reduce heat; cover and simmer for 15 to 20 minutes or until noodles are tender. Remove from heat and top with shredded cheeses; cover and let set until cheese is melted.

GARNISH WITH fresh parsley. ∎

17

18

ONE POT
TURKEY TETRAZZINI

- ¼ C. butter
- 2 tsp. minced garlic
- 16 oz. fresh mushrooms, quartered
- 1 tsp. salt
- ⅛ tsp. cayenne pepper
- 1 C. white grape juice
- ⅓ C. flour
- 5 C. chicken broth
- 16 oz. uncooked spaghetti noodles
- 8 oz. cream cheese, cubed
- 2 to 3 C. cubed cooked turkey
- ½ C. chopped black olives
- 1½ C. frozen green peas
- 1 (8 oz.) jar roasted red peppers, drained
- ¼ C. bacon bits
- 1 C. each shredded Swiss & Romano cheeses

TO BEGIN, melt butter in a pot. Add garlic, mushrooms, salt, and pepper. Cook and stir for 2 minutes. Add juice and cook for 5 minutes. Whisk in flour and cook 1 minute longer. Add broth and uncooked noodles; bring to a boil. Reduce heat and simmer for 8 minutes or until noodles are al dente, stirring occasionally to separate. Add cream cheese and cover until softened. Stir in turkey, olives, frozen peas, roasted peppers, bacon bits, and both cheeses.

GARNISH WITH fresh parsley. ■

19

SLOW-COOKED
CHEESY RAVIOLI

2 (24 oz.) jars 3-cheese pasta sauce

2 (25 oz.) pkgs. frozen beef ravioli

3 C. shredded mozzarella cheese, divided

1 tsp. each garlic salt & Italian seasoning

1½ tsp. onion powder

1 (15 oz.) can tomato sauce

TO BEGIN, coat a slow cooker with cooking spray. Spread 1 cup pasta sauce in the bottom of cooker. Add 1 package frozen ravioli, 1 cup cheese, and half the garlic salt, Italian seasoning, and onion powder. Pour tomato sauce and the remaining pasta sauce from the first jar into cooker. Dump in remaining package of ravioli,

DIRECTIONS CONTINUED ·····················>

One Pot Pastas

20

1 cup cheese, and remaining garlic salt, Italian seasoning, and onion powder. Pour the second jar of pasta sauce over the top. Cover and cook on low for 5 to 6 hours or until ravioli is tender.

TOP WITH remaining 1 cup cheese; cover and let set until melted. ∎

3 qt. pot

UNSTUFFED PEPPERS

22

2 T. olive oil

2 bell peppers, any color, chopped

½ onion, chopped

2 cloves garlic, minced

1 lb. lean ground beef

1 tsp. each coarse salt & pepper

1 (14 oz.) can chicken broth

1 (14.5 oz.) can whole tomatoes, chopped

1 (8 oz.) can tomato sauce

1 tsp. soy sauce

1 C. uncooked long-grain white rice

1 C. shredded Monterey Jack cheese

Sliced green onions

PSST, DIRECTIONS HERE ············

TO BEGIN, heat oil in a pot. Set aside some of the peppers for garnish. Add remaining peppers, onion, and garlic to pot; cook until softened. Add ground beef, salt, and pepper. Cook until meat is done, breaking up meat as it cooks. Add broth, tomatoes, tomato sauce, and soy sauce. Bring to a simmer and stir in rice. Cover pot and reduce heat to low. Cook for 20 to 30 minutes or until rice is tender, stirring occasionally after 20 minutes. Remove from heat, sprinkle with cheese, and cover pot until cheese is melted.

TOP WITH green onions and set-aside bell peppers. ∎

23

6 qt. pot

BEEF STROGANOFF

1 lb. lean ground beef

1½ tsp. minced garlic

⅓ C. flour

¾ C. cream of onion soup

1 (1 oz.) pkg. au jus gravy mix

1 tsp. prepared yellow mustard

8 oz. sliced fresh mushrooms

1 T. salt

16 oz. uncooked old-fashioned wide egg noodles

Water

1 C. sour cream

Splash of dry white wine, optional

TO BEGIN, cook ground beef and garlic in a pot until meat is done, breaking up meat as it cooks. Add flour, stirring to coat meat. Add soup, gravy mix, mustard, mushrooms, salt, uncooked noodles, and enough water to just cover noodles. Bring to a boil. Reduce heat and cook for 15 minutes or until pasta is al dente. Remove from heat.

STIR IN sour cream and wine. ∎

25

3 qt.
pot

MINESTRONE PASTA

2 T. olive oil

1 onion, diced

2 tsp. minced garlic

2 celery ribs, sliced

1 carrot, sliced

1 (28 oz.) can diced
tomatoes

1 (14 oz.) can crushed
tomatoes

1 (15 oz.) can kidney beans,
undrained

2 C. uncooked pipette pasta

1 C. beef broth

1 tsp. each dried oregano,
basil & parsley

1 tsp. salt

½ tsp. pepper

Shredded Cheddar and
Asiago cheeses

26

TO BEGIN, heat oil in a pot. Add onion and cook for 4 minutes or until translucent. Add garlic and cook for 30 seconds. Add celery and carrot; cook for 5 minutes. Add both cans of tomatoes, kidney beans, uncooked pasta, broth, oregano, basil, parsley, salt, and pepper; bring to a boil. Reduce heat to medium and simmer for 10 minutes or until pasta is tender, stirring occasionally.

SPRINKLE WITH both cheeses. ▮

One Pot Pastas

28

CLASSIC PUTTANESCA

1½ tsp. olive oil

1 tsp. minced garlic

2 T. chopped fresh parsley

¼ C. sliced kalamata or stuffed green olives

1 tsp. anchovy paste

1 tsp. dried oregano

½ tsp. cayenne pepper

1 (14.5 oz.) can diced tomatoes

8 oz. uncooked linguini noodles

2 C. chicken stock, plus more as needed

1½ C. dry white wine

1 C. packed arugula

TO BEGIN, heat oil in a pot. Add garlic and cook for 1 minute. Add parsley, olives, anchovy paste, oregano, cayenne pepper, and tomatoes; simmer for 1 minute. Add uncooked noodles, chicken stock, and wine; bring to a boil. Cook on medium heat for 10 minutes or until noodles are al dente, stirring often and adding more chicken stock, if needed. Remove from heat, toss in arugula, and stir to mix.

29

SEASON WITH extra cayenne pepper. ∎

TUNA & NOODLES

30

16 oz. uncooked egg noodles

½ onion, chopped

1 celery rib, sliced

1 C. milk

9 C. water

Garlic powder, salt & pepper to taste

1 (10 oz.) pkg. frozen green peas

¼ C. butter

1 (10.7 oz.) can cream of mushroom soup

1 (12 oz.) can tuna, drained

¼ C. milk

1 C. shredded Cheddar cheese

PSST, DIRECTIONS HERE ··········

TO BEGIN, place uncooked noodles, onion, and celery in a pot. Add milk, water, garlic powder, salt, and pepper. Bring to a boil and cook for 4 minutes, stirring occasionally. Add frozen peas and cook 5 minutes more or until noodles are tender. Remove from heat. Add butter, soup, tuna, milk, and cheese, stirring until cheese is melted.

SEASON WITH extra salt and pepper. ▮

3 qt. skillet

STEAK & NOODLE HOT POT

2 T. canola oil

1 lb. sirloin steak, trimmed & cubed

1 tsp. steak seasoning

Several green onions, sliced

2 cloves garlic, finely chopped

2 (14.5 oz.) cans beef broth

1 (15 oz.) can tomato sauce

8 oz. uncooked campanelle pasta

2 zucchini, cut into matchsticks

2 Roma tomatoes, diced

Shredded Romano cheese

TO BEGIN, heat oil in a skillet. Sprinkle steak with steak seasoning and add to skillet along with onions and garlic. Cook for 5 minutes, stirring occasionally to brown all sides of meat. Add broth and tomato sauce; bring to a boil. Carefully dump in uncooked pasta; reduce heat and simmer for 8 minutes. Add zucchini and simmer for 5 minutes or until crisp-tender. Remove from heat and stir in tomatoes.

33

SPRINKLE WITH cheese and more green onions. ▪

3 qt. pot

CHICKEN ALFREDO
LIGHT

2 C. shredded cooked chicken

Salt & coarse pepper to taste

1 tsp. minced garlic

2 C. chicken broth

1 C. heavy cream

8 oz. uncooked pipette pasta

2 C. shredded Parmesan and/or Romano cheese

1 T. finely chopped fresh parsley

34

PSST, DIRECTIONS HERE·········

TO BEGIN, place chicken, salt, pepper, and garlic in a pot. Stir in broth, cream, and uncooked pasta. Bring to a boil. Cover and reduce heat to a simmer. Cook for 15 to 20 minutes or until pasta is tender. Remove from heat; stir in cheese and parsley.

SPRINKLE WITH more cheese and parsley. ▮

One Pot Pastas

3 qt. pot

36

TURKEY FLORENTINE

3 C. cubed cooked turkey

1 tsp. each salt & pepper

2 T. butter

2 T. olive oil

2 tsp. minced garlic

1 C. dry white wine

1¼ C. chicken broth

8 oz. uncooked pasta shells

2 C. packed fresh baby spinach

1½ C. halved cherry tomatoes

TO BEGIN, season turkey with salt and pepper. Heat butter and oil in a pot until butter is melted. Add turkey and garlic; cook for 30 seconds, stirring constantly. Add wine, broth, and uncooked pasta. Bring to a boil. Reduce heat to a simmer and cook for 15 minutes or until pasta is tender, stirring occasionally. Remove from heat. Stir in spinach and cherry tomatoes.

SEASON WITH extra salt and pepper. ∎

37

BAKED
PIZZA PASTA

8 oz. uncooked rotini pasta

1 (24 oz.) jar spaghetti sauce

2 C. water

1½ tsp. Italian or pizza seasoning

3½ oz. pepperoni slices

1 (2.25 oz.) can sliced black olives, drained

1 green bell pepper, chopped

2 C. shredded mozzarella cheese

TO BEGIN, preheat oven to 350°. Coat a
9 x 13" baking dish with cooking spray and put

DIRECTIONS CONTINUED ·······················>

One Pot Pastas

38

uncooked pasta, spaghetti sauce, water, and Italian seasoning inside; give it a stir. Cover with pepperoni, olives, and bell pepper; top with cheese. Bake for 45 minutes or until hot and bubbly.

GARNISH WITH fresh parsley. ▪

39

5 qt. pot

40

TOMATO-JACK MAC

1 T. butter

1 onion, chopped

2 cloves garlic, finely chopped

16 oz. uncooked elbow macaroni

¼ C. tomato paste

½ tsp. dried oregano

2 tsp. salt

1 tsp. pepper

3½ to 4½ C. milk

1 to 1½ C. shredded Monterey Jack cheese

2 T. grated Parmesan cheese

½ C. sour cream

TO BEGIN, melt butter in a pot. Add onion and garlic; cook until lightly browned. Add uncooked macaroni, tomato paste, oregano, salt, pepper, and enough milk to just cover macaroni; stir to blend. Bring to a boil; reduce heat and simmer for 10 minutes or until macaroni is tender, adding more milk if needed and stirring occasionally. Remove from heat and gradually stir in both cheeses and sour cream.

GARNISH WITH cherry tomatoes. ∎

41

THAI PEANUT POT

1 T. brown sugar

Juice of two limes, divided

12 oz. uncooked fettuccini noodles

4½ C. vegetable broth

2 tsp. minced garlic

1 T. soy sauce

½ tsp. red pepper flakes

½ tsp. grated fresh gingerroot

2 carrots, cut into matchsticks

1 red bell pepper, cut into matchsticks

6 green onions, cut into matchsticks

1 C. salted dry roasted peanuts

2 T. creamy peanut butter

Salt & pepper to taste

1 bunch fresh cilantro, chopped

42

TO BEGIN, in a pot, stir together brown sugar and 1 tablespoon lime juice; add uncooked noodles, broth, garlic, soy sauce, pepper flakes,

DIRECTIONS CONTINUED ·······················>

gingerroot, carrots, bell pepper, green onions, peanuts, and peanut butter. Bring to a boil; cook on medium heat for 10 minutes or until noodles are nearly tender, stirring occasionally. Stir in salt, pepper, and remaining lime juice. Set aside a little cilantro for garnish, then stir remainder into pasta mixture.

GARNISH WITH extra cilantro. ▮

43

3 qt.
slow
cooker

44

SLOW COOKER
TORTELLINI MEATBALL

- 1 (19 oz.) pkg. frozen cheese tortellini
- 1 (26 oz.) pkg. frozen Italian meatballs
- 1 (8 oz.) can tomato sauce
- 1 (24 oz.) jar vodka pasta sauce
- 1 tsp. red pepper flakes
- ½ tsp. each dried basil, marjoram, oregano, rosemary & thyme
- 1 C. water
- Shredded mozzarella cheese

TO BEGIN, spray a slow cooker with cooking spray. Place frozen tortellini and frozen meatballs in cooker; pour tomato and pasta sauces over the top. Sprinkle with pepper flakes, basil, marjoram, oregano, rosemary, and thyme; pour water over all and stir gently. Cover and cook on low for 6 hours or until tortellini is tender.

SPRINKLE WITH cheese and more thyme. ▮

45

SHRIMP PESTO BOWL

12 oz. uncooked penne pasta

1 lb. frozen cooked shrimp

1 (3.5 oz.) jar basil pesto sauce

3 T. chopped sun-dried tomatoes

Salt & pepper to taste

3½ C. chicken broth

2 tsp. instant chicken bouillon granules

¼ C. heavy cream

Feta cheese

TO BEGIN, place uncooked pasta, frozen shrimp, pesto sauce, tomatoes, salt, pepper,

DIRECTIONS CONTINUED ·························>

One Pot Pastas

46

broth, and bouillon granules in a pot. Bring to a boil; cook on medium heat for 6 minutes. Stir in cream and cook 4 minutes more or until pasta is tender.

SPRINKLE WITH cheese. ▪

47

One Pot Pastas

48

ELECTRIC JAMBALAYA

2 T. olive oil

2 onions, chopped

1 green bell pepper, chopped

1 rib celery, sliced

1 (14 oz.) pkg. Andouille sausage, sliced

12 oz. boneless chicken breast, diced

2 (14.5 oz.) cans stewed tomatoes, drained

1½ C. uncooked long-grain white rice

3 C. water

3 tsp. instant chicken bouillon granules

1 to 3 tsp. Cajun or grill seasoning to taste

12 oz. frozen cooked shrimp, thawed

TO BEGIN, heat oil in an electric skillet. Add onions, bell pepper, and celery. Cook for 5 minutes or until softened, stirring occasionally. Stir in sausage, chicken, tomatoes, uncooked rice, water, bouillon granules, Cajun seasoning, and shrimp; bring to a simmer. Cover skillet and cook at 300° for 25 to 30 minutes or until rice is tender.

GARNISH WITH fresh chives. ▌

49

50

MEXICAN ONE-POT MEAL

1 T. olive oil

1 lb. ground pork

1 (15 oz.) can tomato sauce

1 (16 oz.) jar salsa

1⅓ C. uncooked elbow macaroni

1 (12 oz.) bottle Mexican-style beer or beef broth

1 Roma tomato, diced

1 C. frozen whole kernel corn

1 (15 oz.) can black beans, drained & rinsed

1 tsp. salt

½ tsp. pepper

1 C. shredded Mexican cheese blend

Sour cream

PSST, DIRECTIONS HERE ··········

TO BEGIN, heat oil in a pot. Add pork and cook until browned, crumbling meat while cooking. Stir in tomato sauce and salsa. Add uncooked macaroni, beer, tomato, frozen corn, beans, salt, and pepper; stir to combine. Bring to a boil. Reduce heat and simmer for 12 minutes or until macaroni is al dente. Remove from heat and stir in cheese; cover pot until cheese melts.

TOP WITH sour cream and garnish with fresh cilantro. ▌

3 qt. pot

52

CHICKEN LO MEIN

- 1 lb. boneless chicken breast, diced
- 12 oz. uncooked linguini noodles
- 4 carrots, cut into matchsticks
- 1 red bell pepper, cut into matchsticks
- 1 bunch green onions, cut into matchsticks
- 1 C. fresh pea pods, trimmed
- 2 tsp. minced garlic
- ¼ C. soy sauce
- 1 tsp. garlic powder
- 1 tsp. cornstarch
- 1 T. sugar
- ½ tsp. red pepper flakes
- 4 C. chicken broth
- ½ C. water
- 2 tsp. olive oil

TO BEGIN, place chicken, uncooked noodles, carrots, bell pepper, green onions, pea pods, garlic, soy sauce, garlic powder, cornstarch, sugar, pepper flakes, broth, water, and oil in a pot. Bring to a boil. Reduce heat to a simmer, stirring to separate noodles. Cover and cook for 10 minutes; uncover and cook 5 minutes more or until noodles are tender.

GARNISH WITH sliced green onions. ∎

53

BUFFALO CHICKEN
HOT POT

3 C. milk

1 C. heavy cream

1 C. chicken stock

2 T. butter

1½ tsp. dry mustard

1½ tsp. salt

16 oz. uncooked pasta shells

1 C. shredded Cheddar cheese

1 C. shredded smoked Gouda cheese

½ C. blue cheese crumbles

¾ to 1 C. buffalo wing sauce to taste

2 C. cubed cooked chicken breast

Pepper to taste

TO BEGIN, combine milk, cream, chicken stock, butter, dry mustard, salt, and uncooked pasta in a pot. Bring to a simmer, stirring frequently. Reduce heat to low. Cook for 10 minutes or until pasta

DIRECTIONS CONTINUED ·······················>

is al dente, stirring frequently. Remove from heat, stir in all three cheeses, wing sauce, chicken, and pepper. Cover for 5 minutes or until cheese is melted; stir. Add more milk or cream to desired thickness.

SEASON WITH pepper. ∎

3 qt. skillet

GARDEN

BACON CHEESEBURGER
SKILLET

12 bacon strips

1 lb. lean ground beef

Seasoned salt & black pepper to taste

¼ C. chopped onion

2 (15 oz.) cans tomato sauce

2 C. beef broth

1 C. water

16 oz. uncooked rotini pasta

6 Roma tomatoes, diced

1 (14.5 oz.) can diced tomatoes

¼ C. ketchup

2 T. spicy brown mustard

1 C. shredded Cheddar cheese

TO BEGIN, brown bacon and ground beef in a hot skillet, crumbling meat as it cooks; sprinkle with seasoned salt and pepper. Add onion, tomato sauce, broth, water, uncooked pasta, all the tomatoes, ketchup, and mustard; give it a quick stir and bring to a boil. Reduce heat and simmer for 10 minutes or until pasta is al dente, stirring occasionally. Remove from heat and gently stir in cheese.

SPRINKLE WITH more cheese. ∎

57

SALMON-DILL PASTA

1 (1 lb.) salmon fillet, about 1" thick

8 oz. uncooked thin spaghetti noodles

½ C. dry white wine

1 shallot, finely chopped

Water

1 lb. fresh asparagus, trimmed
   & cut into 1" pieces

3 T. lemon juice

4 tsp. capers, rinsed

1 (4 oz.) jar pimentos, drained

½ C. sour cream

1 T. salt

⅛ to ¼ tsp. cayenne pepper to taste

¼ tsp. white pepper

1 tsp. lemon pepper

¼ C. chopped fresh dill

One Pot Pastas

58

TO BEGIN, place salmon, uncooked noodles, wine, and shallot in a pot. Add enough water to just cover salmon and noodles. Bring to a boil, stirring to separate noodles. Reduce heat to a simmer, cover, and cook for 4 minutes.

DIRECTIONS CONTINUED ·······················>

Add asparagus and cook
3 minutes more or until
asparagus is crisp-tender
and noodles are al dente.
Stir in lemon juice, capers,
and pimentos. Remove
from heat. Add sour cream,
salt, cayenne pepper, white
pepper, lemon pepper, and
dill. Stir to combine and
break apart salmon.

TOP WITH more dill. ∎

59

One Pot Pastas

3 qt. skillet

60

SPICY
SAUSAGE SKILLET

- 1 T. olive oil
- 1 (13 oz.) pkg. smoked sausage links, sliced
- 1½ C. diced onion
- 1 tsp. minced garlic
- 2 C. chicken broth
- 1 (10 oz.) can tomatoes with green chilies
- ½ C. heavy cream
- 8 oz. uncooked penne pasta
- ½ tsp. each salt & pepper
- 1 C. shredded Monterey Jack cheese, divided

TO BEGIN, heat oil in a skillet. Add sausage and onion; cook until lightly browned. Add garlic and cook for 30 seconds. Stir in broth, tomatoes, cream, uncooked pasta, salt, and pepper. Bring to a boil. Reduce heat, cover, and simmer for 15 minutes or until pasta is tender. Remove from heat and stir in ½ cup Monterey Jack cheese. Top with remaining ½ cup cheese and cover skillet until melted.

GARNISH WITH green onions. ∎

61

One Pot Pastas

3 qt. pot

62

ITALIAN
WEDDING SOUP PASTA

2 T. olive oil

1 onion, finely chopped

2 celery ribs, thinly sliced

2 carrots, thinly sliced

1 tsp. salt

3 C. chicken broth, divided

3 C. coarsely chopped fresh spinach

8 oz. uncooked pasta rings

24 precooked meatballs *(purchased or homemade)*

Shredded Parmesan cheese

TO BEGIN, heat oil in a pot. Add onion, celery, and carrots; cook for 5 minutes or until softened, stirring occasionally. Add salt and 1 cup broth; bring to a boil. Stir in spinach, uncooked pasta, and remaining 2 cups broth. Bring to a boil. Reduce heat and simmer for 10 minutes or until pasta is al dente. Add meatballs during last few minutes of cooking time to heat through.

63

SPRINKLE WITH cheese. ▪

INDEX

So, what are one pot pastas?

Simply start with a pot and a lovely jumble of ingredients. Drizzle in the liquids and let it all simmer into an amazing collection of flavors. No pre-boiling the pasta – ever!

No straining. No draining.
No dirtying more than one pot.

Just combine, cook, and eat.
So easy. So quick. So delicious.

Item # 7120
Made in USA

ISBN 978-1-56383-500-1

9 781563 835001 >